MW00990762

100 AUTHENTIC BLUES HARMONICA Licks

★ BY STEVE COHEN ★

All harmonica and guitar played by Steve Cohen.
Steve Cohen can be found through his website www.stevecohenblues.com.

Back cover photo: Francis Ford

ISBN 978-1-4803-1291-3

HAL•LEONARD® CORPORATION

7777 W. BLUEMOUND RD. P.O. BOX 13819 MILWAUKEE, WI 53213

In Australia Contact:
Hal Leonard Australia Pty. Ltd.
4 Lentara Court
Cheltenham, Victoria, 3192 Australia
Email: ausadmin@halleonard.com.au

Visit Hal Leonard Online at
www.halleonard.com

CONTENTS

INTRODUCTION

As of the writing of this book, blues music has been around for about 150 years. As times have changed, so has blues, and all contemporary music. Early blues was created from a composite of musical styles. Many expressions of blues can be traced to African musical traditions, but adaptations of European religious music, American work songs, and other multi-ethnic styles were also parts of the mix.

Many original musical and lyrical characteristics of blues music are retained as the music evolves. Certain musical elements, such as often re-used musical phrases, or licks, have survived to become the basis for much present day blues music. This book undertakes to present 100 of these authentic musical phrases, to be played on the harmonica. Many are original to the harmonica; others have been adapted over the years for the harmonica, and others are just a natural fit for this instrument.

One characteristic of the process by which original blues music is created has to do with sharing or borrowing not only phrases from lyrics, but also musical phrases. Some of these licks have become the basis for numerous standard blues songs. It's hard to say which came first in many instances. Were songs created using these licks as their basis, or were the licks extracted from pre-existing songs? There's a "chicken or the egg" conundrum here, to which the answer is largely irrelevant for our purposes. What matters here is that these are highly recognizable, and often repeated, musical phrases that partially form the basis for the blues as we know it. Very often, licks that are an important element of a song appear in other songs—sometimes several other songs—and these licks are certainly used as elements in soloing on harmonica and other instruments.

Traditionally, blues harmonica players have gradually assimilated these licks as their personal styles developed. These important repertoire builders are gathered together here for the first time.

Even though this book is targeted specifically for harmonica, these licks can be, and often are, played by guitar, piano, and saxophone, and also form the basis for the partial or complete melody lines of many blues songs, both vocal and instrumental.

UNDERSTANDING BLUES PROGRESSIONS—WHY AND HOW

Presenting these cool and authentic blues licks on the harmonica is a basic goal of this book. However, the licks are just the building blocks of blues harmonica playing. To apply these licks to the real world of playing with other musicians, it's important to understand the musical mechanics of the basic 12-bar blues chord progression.

Your key of C harmonica is usually played in one of three keys: C: 1st position, G: 2nd position, or D: 3rd position. Coincidentally, these are the same three chords that make up a 12-bar blues progression in the key of G. To make the most of the information in this book, it might become important to gain an understanding of how and where to apply these licks in a 12-bar blues song.

There are numerous variations of the basic 12-bar blues progression, but at its most basic, it looks like this:

Bar:	1	2	3	4	5	6	7	8	9	10	11	12
Chord Value:	I	I	I	I	IV	IV	I	I	V	IV	I	I
Chord Name in Key of G:	G	G	G	G	C	C	G	G	D	C	G	G

One logical and effective way to apply blues licks to blues progressions is to use as a foundation a simple lick, and then transpose it over the three chords of a 12-bar blues progression. You can add embellishments, ornaments, and/or more notes or effects, but transposing is a great way to apply licks to solos or accompaniments. Many of the licks exemplified in this book have been transposed over the basic blues chord changes.

All examples in this book will be played on a 10-hole diatonic harmonica in the key of C. Unless otherwise noted, examples are in 2nd position. Examples in 1st or 3rd position will be labeled as such.

AN ASSORTMENT OF BLUES GROOVE LICKS

ASCENDING SWING LICK AND VARIATIONS

1 Here's a lick that is a basic ingredient of many others. It can be used almost anywhere in a blues shuffle progression, and is a great launching point for a solo. This lick is often part of a lick that develops further. Notice the small notes in parentheses above the musical staff. This tells you to swing your eighth notes.

AUDIO
TRACK
1

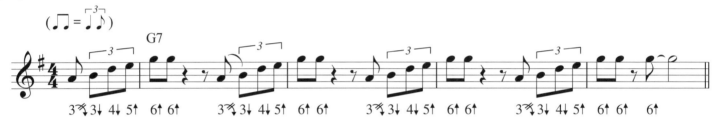

1A The lick above is played in the lower register. It also sounds good in the upper register where it can be played in single notes or tongue-blocked octaves.

AUDIO
TRACK
1 (cont.)

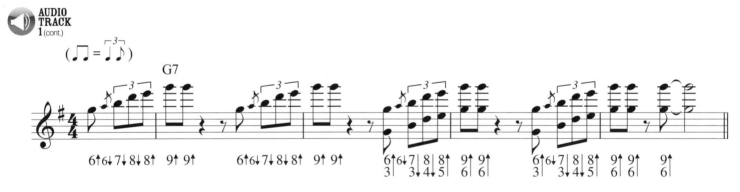

1B There are countless ways to extend, alter, or embellish this basic line. Here are a couple of licks that use this phrase as its foundation.

AUDIO
TRACK
1 (cont.)

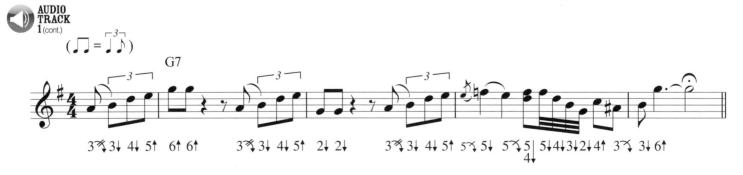

1C

Here's a 3rd position version of the basic ascending swing lick. Many licks are often executed in this harmonica cross. In this example, your C harmonica will be played in the key of D.

1D

Adding a few notes to the previous 3rd position lick gives it another feel.

2

Here is another extended version of the ascending swing lick. This lick gets played with a combination of single-note puckers and tongue-block chords. James Cotton has used this one.

3 Little Walter, James Cotton, and Paul Butterfield all liked to use versions of this lick. It works well as a fill or response lick and is another extended version of the ascending swing lick.

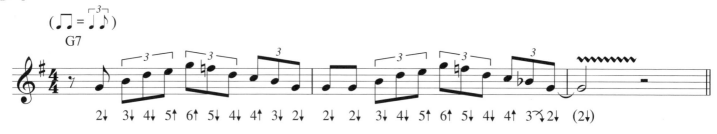

BOOGIE-WOOGIE BASED LICKS

4 This lick is another phrase that forms the basic pattern for numerous others. Boogie-woogie was originally developed by piano players, but has come to be played by many instruments in many songs. It's among the most prevalent families of blues licks. This is usually played with a shuffle feel, and there are numerous ways to play it. This basic version is easily transposed over the changes of a 12-bar.

5 This lick is a variation of boogie-woogie that comes through in many other songs as a background part. Transposing this lick over the chords of a blues progression is easily accomplished, and as such, it makes a great lick for background playing or a launching point for a solo.

AUDIO
TRACK
6 (includes play-along section)

6 Here's another variation that uses most of the same notes in almost the same order, but with a slight change in rhythm. Variations of this appear in many other blues songs.

This variation is easily transposed over the chords of a 12-bar, and as such makes another good background part or basis for soloing.

AUDIO
TRACK
7 (includes play-along section)

7 This phrase is another great example of a variation of boogie-woogie that's been incorporated into the compendium of blues licks. This lick is a natural for transposing over all three chords of a 12-bar.

AUDIO TRACK 8

7A In the previous example, the harp moves into a lower register to accommodate the IV chord and V chord changes, and to maintain melodic integrity. To keep moving chromatically upward with the chord changes, you could employ an over-blow (indicated by a circle above the bend arrow) in the licks that are played over the IV and V chords. The upward moving transition between chords might sound more natural played like this. If nothing else, it provides some options.

AUDIO TRACK 8 (includes play-along section)

8 Here's another variation of boogie-woogie. It involves jumping from a 3 draw to a 7 draw, which makes it a good exercise for getting a feel for the distance between those two notes. Since you can't look at the harp while you're playing it, you need to develop a feel for the distances between holes.

AUDIO TRACK 9

STOP-TIME LICKS

9 Among the most popular of blues licks, this one is a natural for harmonica. It works well with songs like "Mannish Boy," "I'm Your Hoochie Coochie Man," "Bad to the Bone," "I'm a Man," and many others. There are plenty of ways to play this, and here are three of them. The first two versions are played here with single notes, while the third is played with tongue-blocked chords.

AUDIO TRACK 10

9A The previous lick is a natural to play in 1st position, and was originally recorded this way. This next example is played on a C harp, in the key of C.

First position has some great attributes. Playing in 1st position over the V chord is like playing in 2nd position over the I chord. First position also has great potential over the I chord in the upper register, where the blow note bends extend the chromatic note selection. There are examples of some 1st position high note licks later in this book.

10 This phrase works well as a response lick in stop-time songs like "Boom Boom," "I Done Got over It," or "I'm Your Hoochie Coochie Man."

11 This two-part lick is a variation and extension of the previous lick. It works well in songs like "Shake Your Hips" or "I Hate to See You Go." These two alternating licks form their own kind of call and response.

12 Though timed differently, this lick bears melodic similarity to the first stop-time lick. There's a "bounce back" feature between the 1 draw- and 2 draw-second bend. This makes a great background segment, launching point for a solo, or repetitive lick over the I chord.

12A You can add what I refer to as a trill (See the beginning of beats 2 and 4.) as a sort of ornament to the previous lick to give it a little more interest.

12B This lick sounds good played in octaves and chords.

12C You can also use octaves and chords to play it in the upper register.

DESCENDING INTERVAL LICKS

13 Based on descending intervals, this phrase works well as a bridge between other sections of solos. It's a four note run with the first two notes doubled. The recorded example has a little bit of lick 12a tagged onto the end.

14 This is a two-note lick that employs the descending interval. It could be played starting with the 10-hole draw and descending the entire length of the instrument, or any section thereof. Having control over this and the next two licks provides a versatile tool for creating fluid solos.

15 Here's a descending interval lick using triplets. This is the same deal as the last lick: it could begin anywhere starting with the 10-hole draw on down.

16 This four-note descending interval lick could also start with the 10-hole draw and work its way down the entire instrument.

17 This lick uses descending intervals as its basis, though the timing is a lot bluesier. It sounds like something Big Bill Broonzy would play on guitar, but Little Walter liked this lick and used versions of it. It's played here with a combination of tongue-block chords and single notes.

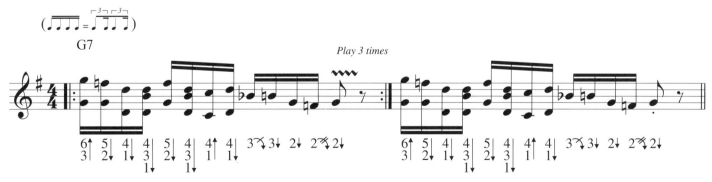

ASCENDING INTERVAL LICKS

18 Lick 13 above also works well in a solo when played in reverse, from the bottom of the harp up.

AUDIO
TRACK
19

19 This ascending lick has a bounce back in it. This makes a great turnaround lick, but has plenty of other applications.

AUDIO
TRACK
20

FUNK LICKS

20 Here is another lick that is the foundation for a whole family of blues licks. This lick fits well over a funk beat. It works well with songs from the New Orleans school of blues and also in numerous funk groove blues tunes. Notice that the eighth notes are not swung this time.

AUDIO
TRACK
21

21 You can create a related funky lick if you add a note to the beginning of the last example and change the beat around a little. The abbreviation "sim." refers to the staccatos in the previous measure. Play those eighths short throughout the lick. This lick fits nicely as a background part or for solo-building in the family of songs that includes tunes like "You Belong to Me," "Tramp," or "If You Love Me Like You Say." This one is easy to transpose over all the blues changes.

AUDIO TRACK
21 (includes play-along section)

22 Another familiar lick that transposes easily over the three changes of a blues progression is shown below. It works well in songs like "Just a Little Bit," "I Don't Play," and "Woke Up This Morning," among others.

AUDIO TRACK
22 (includes play-along section)

23 Here's another great lick to use with a funk or swamp beat. There's more than one way to play this, but this version combines single notes with chords and contains a couple of glissandos. It plays easily over the changes of a 12-bar.

AUDIO TRACK 23

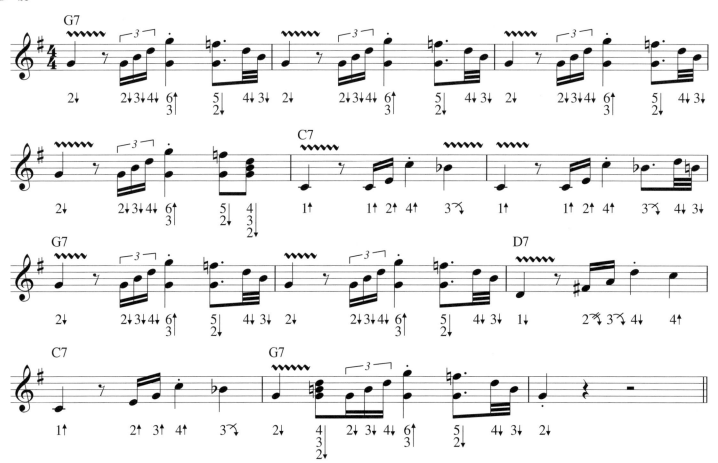

24 Some licks feel as percussive as they are melodic. This staccato riff, sometimes called the "chicken scratch," can be used for punctuation in a solo and works well in any funky song.

AUDIO TRACK 23 (includes play-along section)

25 This is another classic lick, sometimes used as a bass or guitar part, as in "Snatch It Back and Hold It," "Messin' with the Kid," or "Flower Blues." There's a little bounce back element to it and is another good one for transposing over blues changes.

AUDIO TRACK **24** (includes play-along section)

26 Here's another classic lick that gets played a lot. It's sometimes used repetitively as a verse-ending motif.

AUDIO TRACK **25**

27 If you isolate the last four notes of lick 26, a descending sequence exists that is the basis for some other familiar licks. Sometimes favored by Little Walter, this one might fit better over a mojo beat (2 feel) than a funk beat.

AUDIO TRACK **25** (cont.)

27A
This lick is an extension of the previous one. It doubles the ending section, which gives it a different feel, and works well as a turnaround or as a stand-alone lick.

AUDIO
TRACK
25 (cont.)

SHUFFLE LICKS

28
Another lick that is the foundation for a family of versatile phrases, this one has a bounce back in it. It works well with songs like "I'm Ready," "Doodlin'," or "Keep on Loving Me Baby." It makes an apt and authentic repetitive background part in many different blues songs, and can be played over all the 12-bar blues changes without alteration.

AUDIO
TRACK
26

28A You can throw a little trill into this to give it more color.

28B The previous lick also gets played frequently in 3rd position. This example will be played on a C harmonica in the key of D.

Little Walter was a pioneer of 3rd-position blues playing, and sometimes used the chromatic harmonica as his instrument of choice for this cross, as the note sequence is the same as on a diatonic harp.

28C

This 3rd position version sounds good played in tongue-blocked chords. This example uses the chord "tongue waggle" (trill) on the last note of each phrase that is described later in lick 60.

AUDIO
TRACK
27 (cont.)

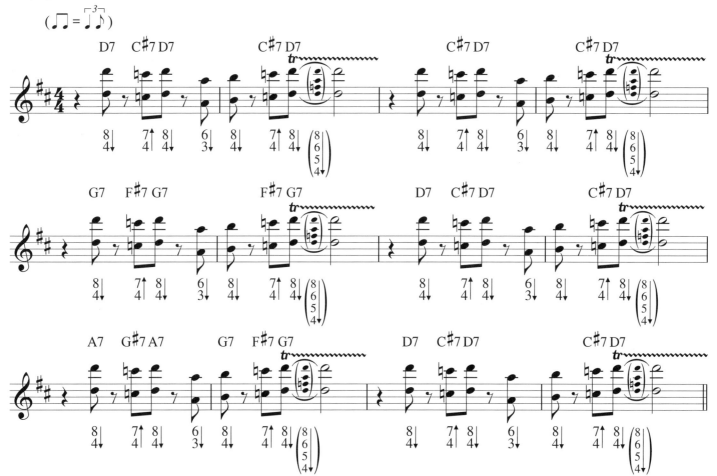

28D

A slight change in timing of the above 3rd-position lick creates a phrase that offers a good way to move from the high register down to the low end of the harp. It makes a good verse ending lick in 3rd position, or an authentic stand-alone lick over the I chord.

AUDIO
TRACK
27 (cont.)

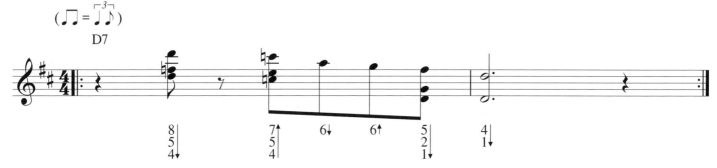

29
The next lick makes a good intro phrase over the I chord, but can be used over all the changes of a blues progression. It's an easy single-note lick.

AUDIO TRACK 28

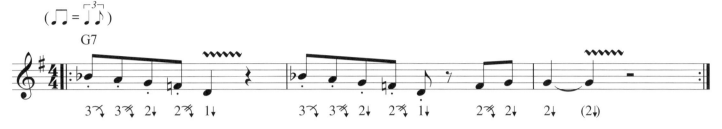

29A
As a variation, you can add a little bounce back to fill it out.

AUDIO TRACK 28 (cont.)

29B
This version of the above lick employs the bounce back concept over three descending intervals, and makes for a nifty lick.

AUDIO TRACK 28 (cont.)

30 Here's an authentic lick that's played in tongue-blocked chords. It works best played over the I chord.

AUDIO TRACK 29

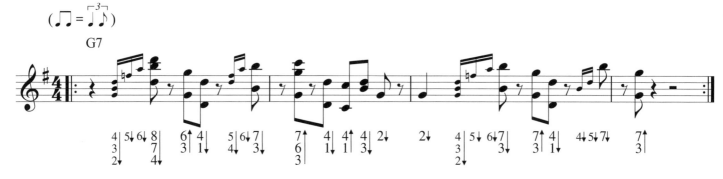

31 Here's another authentic lick that pops up a lot and is worth knowing. It works well as a launching point for a solo, and also as a background part on any number of blues shuffle tunes. This example is played in single notes.

AUDIO TRACK 30

31A The previous lick also sounds good played with tongue-blocked chords. This example is played first with chords and octaves in the low register, then with tongue-block chords in the high register.

AUDIO TRACK 30 (cont.)

31B

Lick 31 works well in 3rd position. In this example, your C harp will be played in the key of D, first in the high register, then in the low register.

32

Here's another lick that is found in many variations in several blues songs. It can be played without transposition over all the blues changes of a 12-bar. I'm playing it here using tongue-block chords. There are double stops on the first notes of each phrase.

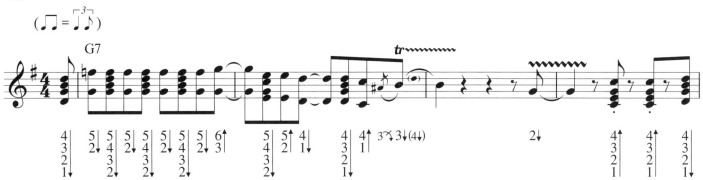

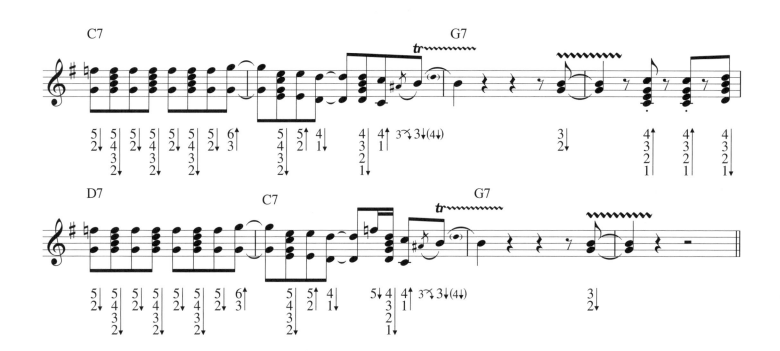

32A The previous lick was played in the lower register. This example is repeated in the high register.

AUDIO TRACK
32 (includes play-along section)

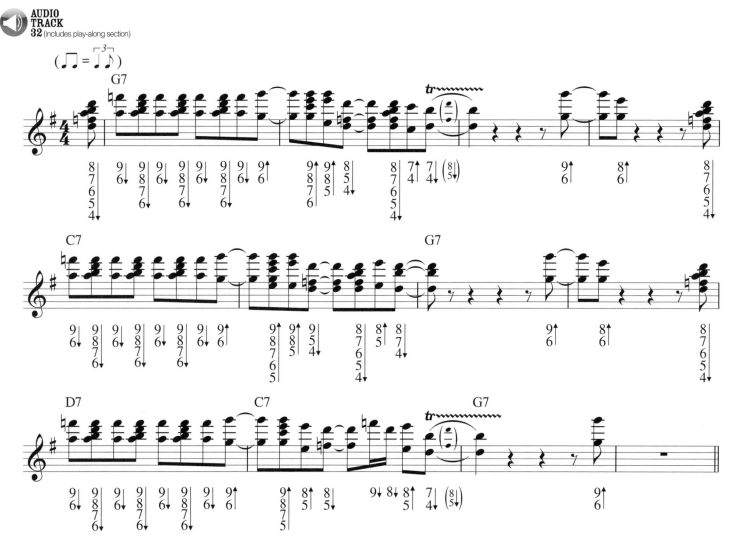

33
This sequence of licks works well in 8-bar blues tunes. For a unique approach, you can bend down the 2-draw a whole step (2nd bend) while you're playing the 3/2 draw chord at the end of the second phrase. This makes the lick stand out.

AUDIO TRACK 33 (includes play-along section)

34
One of the most frequently used blues licks of all time, this classic was probably first played on the guitar, but translates well to harmonica. It can be found in songs recorded by Elmore James, but reaches back to Robert Johnston and beyond. "Sweet Home Chicago" and "Dust My Broom" are among the best known songs that contain this universal lick.

AUDIO TRACK 34

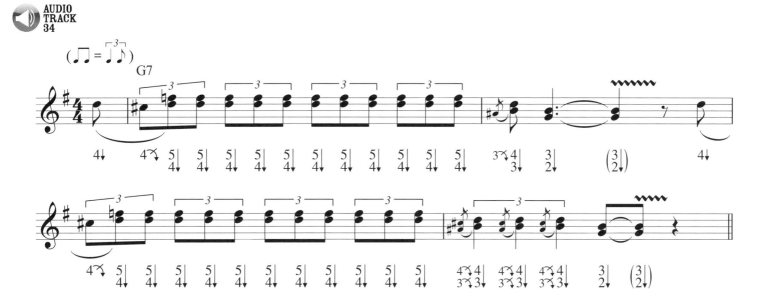

35
Here's a bass or guitar lick that's often heard on harmonica. It's a staple, and can be used as a fill, background part, or part of a solo.

AUDIO TRACK 35

36
This lick and its variations are found in a whole family of songs. Willie Cobb, Magic Sam, Junior Wells, and Little Walter are among the artists that liked to use versions of this lick. It's most often played over a shuffle beat. The first example is played in the low register.

AUDIO TRACK 36

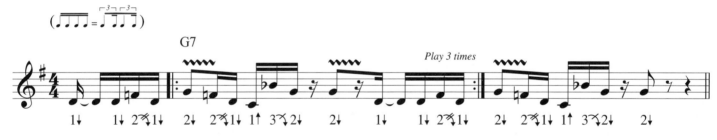

36A
This example is a variation of lick 36 played in the middle register.

AUDIO TRACK 36 (cont.)

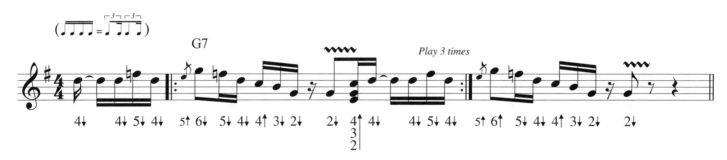

36B You can combine these two licks to form a more complete line.

36C If you change the rhythm around a little, a very similar lick is created, one that Jimi Hendrix liked to use. It's a great example of the timelessness of certain blues phrases.

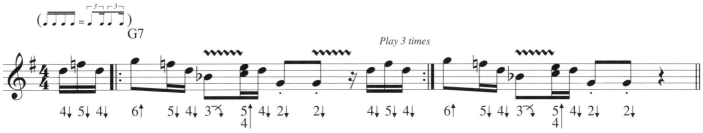

36D

Lick 36 is often played in 3rd position, which puts your C harp in the key of D. This three-part example is first played in the lower register with single notes, then in the upper register using single notes, and finally, in the upper register using chords and tongue-block octaves.

AUDIO TRACK 37

HORN RIFFS ADAPTED FOR HARMONICA

37

James Cotton liked to play this lick. It probably originated on saxophone, but sounds great on harmonica. It works well with jump blues tunes, and can be played over 12-bar changes without much alteration.

AUDIO TRACK 38

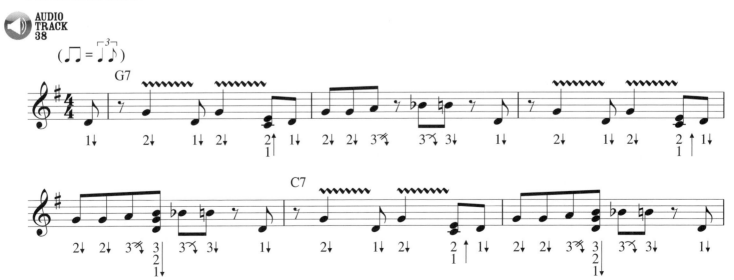

37A
You can play a version of the previous lick using tongue-blocked octaves and chords. There is an accommodation over the IV and V chords.

AUDIO TRACK
38 (includes play-along section)

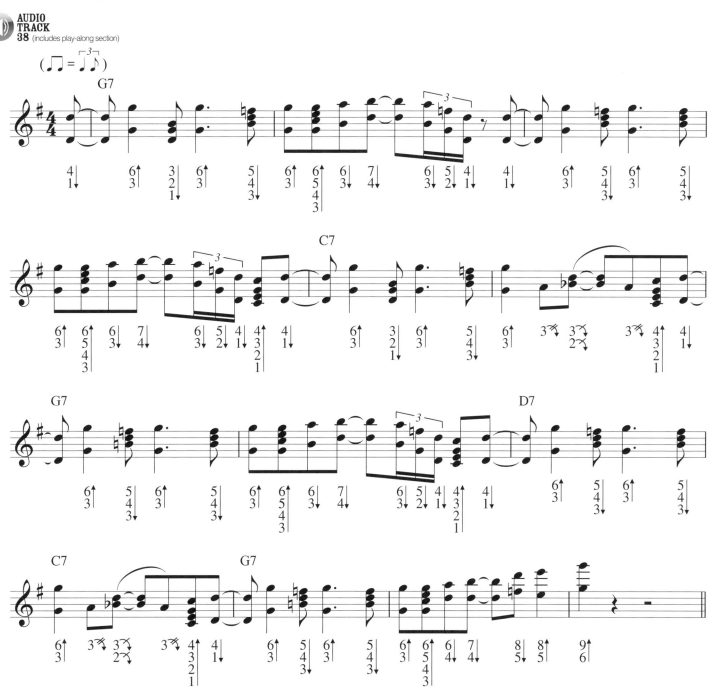

38 Here's another classic horn lick that sounds good on harmonica. It is pretty easily transposed over all the blues changes. It sounds good in tunes "Juke," "Soulful Drums," or just about any shuffle tune.

AUDIO TRACK **39** (includes play-along section)

39 This next example employs a bounce back and is applicable to numerous blues songs. It works well with the jazz/blues standards "Red Top," "One Thing Leads to Another," and "Going to Chicago" among others, but is a great multipurpose lick for background parts or soloing. Transposition requires only minor adaptation for playing over the changes of a 12-bar.

AUDIO TRACK **40**

40 From the same melodic family of licks as the previous two, this lick also probably originated as a horn riff. It works well with most 12-bar mid tempo swing shuffles. It's easily transposed over the blues changes.

AUDIO
TRACK
41 (includes play-along section)

41 This is a horn riff from the swing band era. James Cotton used this lick, as do many other blues harmonica players.

AUDIO
TRACK
42

41A Here is an adaptation of the previous stock phrase. This is a lick that Little Walter used. There is a double stop toward the beginning.

42 Another horn lick from the swing era that sounds great on harmonica, this one makes a good chorus ending lick, plays nicely over the I chord, or makes a good tension building lick releasing into the IV chord in the fourth bar of a blues progression.

42A In this variation of the previous lick, the resolution notes are played with over-blows in the middle register.

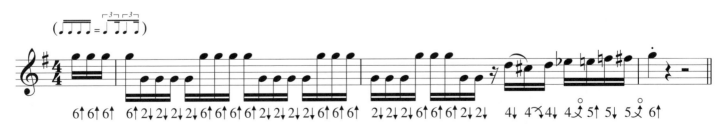

TECHNIQUE LICKS

RHYTHM AND REPEATING LICKS

Harmonica music is produced by both inhaling and exhaling, and because of this unique feature, it is possible to play certain licks repeatedly without having to alter your breathing. Here are some licks that take advantage of this feature.

43 This classic, short lick can be played over any of the blues changes, and gets used a lot by Junior Wells among others. Played repeatedly, it makes a good showstopper, but also has application as a solo fragment.

44 It's good to have a bag of tricks or licks that you can tastefully utilize once or twice a night. Here is a speed lick to interject over the I chord. You can play it slowly, double-time it, or play it at any tempo of your choosing. It's based on a country fiddle phrase, but it works well as a blues lick.

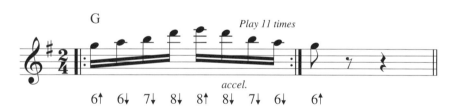

45 Here's a great repeating lick that's played using tongue-block chords and octaves. It works best over the I chord. Like the last lick, you can alter the tempo at will.

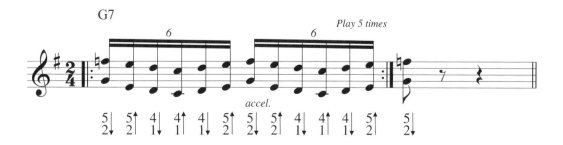

45A Here's the same lick played in the upper register, also with tongue-block chords.

AUDIO TRACK 46 (cont.)

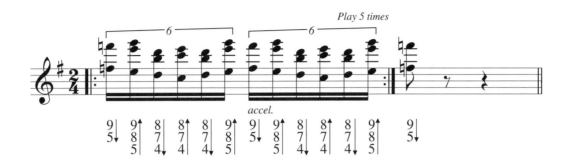

46 Once you have control over the 2nd bend on the 2-hole draw, this makes an effective repetitive lick.

AUDIO TRACK 47

47 Next is a variation of lick 46. One note has been removed, which creates a very different rhythmic feel.

AUDIO TRACK 48

48 This makes a good repeating lick for one-chord harp jams. It works well over songs like "Parchman Farm" and "Another Man Done Gone." John Mayall used this lick a lot. It alternates between chords and single notes.

AUDIO TRACK 49

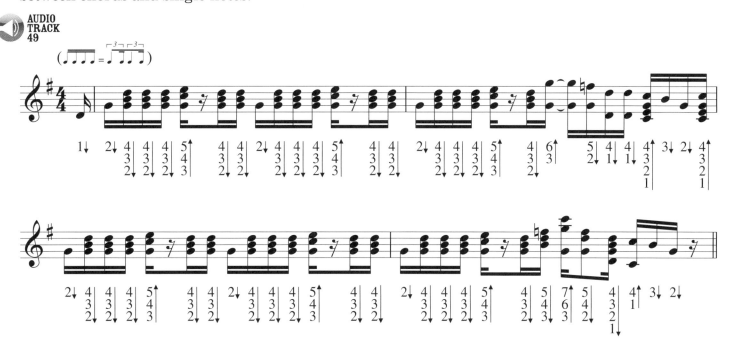

49 Many of these repetitive licks can be thought of as being percussive. There's more than one way to play the next one. It is a common lick to use over what is sometimes called the "mojo beat," and also works well as a background on songs like "Got My Mo Jo Working," "I Got to Go," or "She's Murder" among many others. By tagging on a standard turnaround, it works well over 12-bar changes, although you could power all the way through a chorus without adding a thing.

AUDIO TRACK 50

49A Here's another classic breathing pattern lick that gets used repeatedly over a mojo beat. It makes a great option as a background part over this family of songs.

50 This repetitive triplet speed lick can be adapted to play over the three chords of a 12-bar. It is based on a triplet.

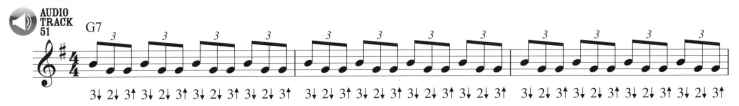

51 Another great repeating speed lick, this one makes a good showstopper in a solo. It can be played over all the changes of a 12-bar and bears similarity to the previous lick, but with an extra note in the repetitions. This is a high-speed bounce back lick that requires good control over the incremental bends.

AUDIO
TRACK
51 (includes play-along section)

WARBLE LICKS

One frequently employed blues harmonica technique is sometimes called the warble, or the shake. This trilling technique involves moving back and forth between two adjacent holes to create a sound that is somewhere between a chord and a tremolo effect. It's possible to play the 4(5)-draw warble at any place in a 12-bar blues chord progression and sound melodically correct. Simply playing an extended warble continuously can be considered a lick in itself, and is used frequently in slow blues solos, as well as in other ways.

The warble can be done at a variety of speeds, and on any two adjacent reeds. It is a technique that can be used as a treatment for any individual note, much like you can add vibrato or glissando to help bring phrases to life.

52 This lick has a chromatic flavor. It sounds excellent to transpose this over the three chords of a 12-bar. It makes for great bending practice to execute the incremental bends while playing this warble lick over the IV and V chords.

AUDIO
TRACK
52 (includes play-along section)

53 Little Walter liked to use this next one. It works well in songs with the Bo Diddley beat like "Roller Coaster," "Pretty Thing," or "Mona." Slowed down, it sounds good played in a slow blues song.

54 This is another lick that Little Walter liked to use. It works well over the I chord as is.

55 This lick approximates the blues guitar lick sometimes called the "lumpety lump," or Jimmy Reed shuffle. Despite being thought of as a guitar lick, it sounds great on harmonica. It makes a nice basis for a one-chord harp jam.

55A Adding a couple of notes to the end of the previous phrase creates a great lick that works well as a breathing exercise. This works well in songs like "Big Boss Man," "You Don't Have to Go," or any Jimmy Reed-type shuffle tune.

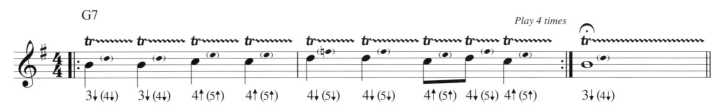

55B Playing the same notes but with a swing feel changes the flavor of this next lick. James Cotton liked to use this. It is less a warble lick than a straight chord lick, but is melodically similar to the lumpety lump.

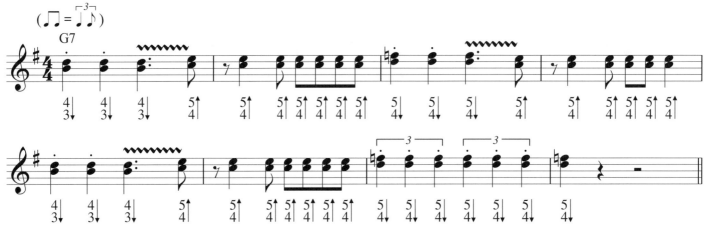

56 James Cotton liked to use this version of a nice descending lick. It combines a lumpety lump with some warbles. It is played here with chords with a warble, which adds to the difficulty factor.

56A Here is an adaptation of the previous lick that can be employed repetitively over the I chord.

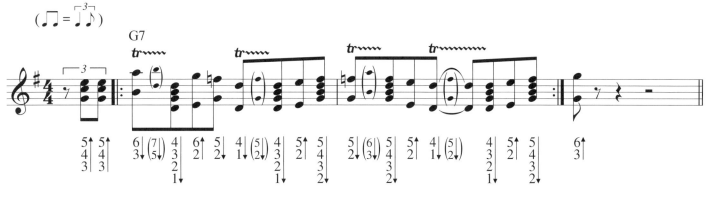

57 Another classic lick that Little Walter liked to use is played here, accurately transposed over the blues changes. This works well with slow blues songs. When sped up, it bears a similarity to lick 54. The difficulty factor is increased by virtue of having a warble with a bend in the section that's played over the V chord.

AUDIO
TRACK
57 (includes play-along section)

58
This lick works well as a transition from the I chord to the IV chord. The example is played first in single notes, then warble is added for extra flavor. The warble increases the difficulty, as it takes good control of the incremental bends to execute this short phrase.

59
This ascending run could be played with single notes, but adding warbles to every note makes it more interesting. Playing it with warbles also adds to the difficulty of execution.

FLUTTER CHORD TREMOLO

The "fluttery chord tremolo" is a classic harp technique. Much like the warble, it can be employed continuously over an individual chord as a stand-alone lick, often in slow blues tunes. It's a kind of vibrato, executed by waggling the tongue while playing a chord, and can be added to any chord or octave for extra effect.

60 This flutter lick is wrapped up in lead-in notes and resolution notes.

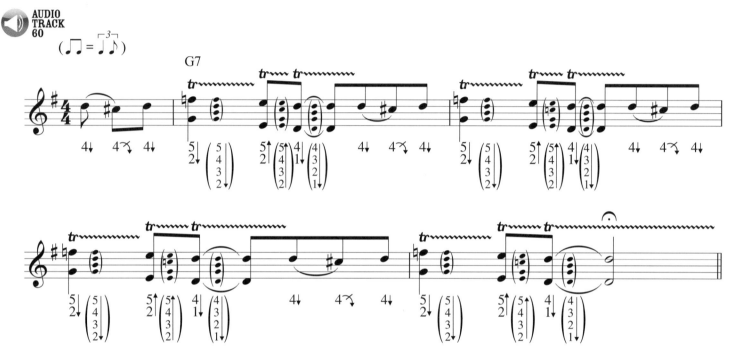

60A The fluttery chord technique can be used as a tremolo effect any time you are playing a tongue-blocked chord or octave. This descending interval lick employs the flutter as it descends all the way down the harp.

GLISSANDO LICKS

Because of the way the harmonica is laid out, glissando is an easily executed, natural sounding technique that can add some flavor to your licks. Harmonica glissando involves sliding from a starting note and quickly passing through an adjacent note, or several notes, before settling on the targeted ending note. This technique can also be used in the middle of a lick. Glissando can be used in much the same way you can add vibrato, warble, or flutter to existing licks.

61 This is a great lick with a gliss in the beginning. It sounds best over the I chord, but could be played all the way through a 12-bar progression.

62 This lick ends with a gliss.

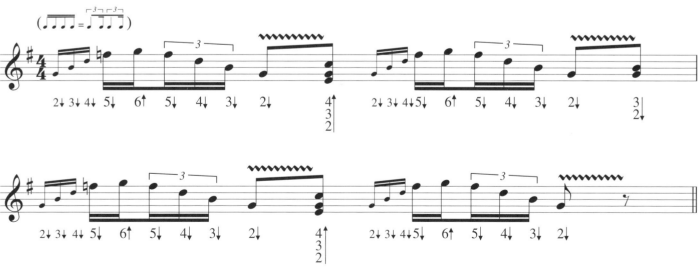

63 Here is a glissando lick that descends from the top of the harp. You can achieve a cascading effect by targeting a starting note and adding a gliss with each interval.

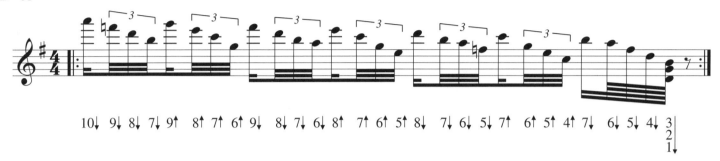

10↓ 9↓ 8↓ 7↓ 9↑ 8↑ 7↑ 6↑ 9↓ 8↓ 7↓ 6↓ 8↑ 7↑ 6↑ 5↑ 8↓ 7↓ 6↓ 5↓ 7↑ 6↑ 5↑ 4↑ 7↓ 6↓ 5↓ 4↓ 3↓ 2↓ 1↓

64 This lick could be in the section on repeating licks. It's possible to repeat this one indefinitely because the breathing is so balanced.

1↓ 2↓ 3↓ 4↓ 1↑ 2↑ 3↑ 4↑ 1↓ 2↓ 3↓ 4↓ 1↑ 2↑ 3↑ 4↑ 1↓ 2↓ 3↓ 4↓ 1↑ 2↑ 3↑ 4↑ 1↓ 2↓ 3↓ 4↓ 1↑ 2↑ 3↑ 4↑   1↓

BLUES PROGRESSION LICKS

LICKS SUITABLE FOR TRANSPOSING OVER THE THREE CHORDS OF A BLUES PROGRESSION

65 Here's a simple lick that transposes easily over blues changes.

AUDIO TRACK 65 (includes play-along section)

66 Here's an easy, classic lick with a chromatic section. It works well transposed over all the chords of a 12-bar. This version is played on the low end of the harp. It does some register jumping to stay true to the melody (moving down over the IV and V chords). It should be noted that although this lick is transposed in this example, it is often played over the blues chord changes without alteration, and it sounds ok that way.

AUDIO TRACK 66

66A This is a harmony of the previous lick and is played in the middle register. In the interest of staying harmonically correct and moving into a higher register as the chords move higher, it employs a couple of over-blows.

AUDIO TRACK 66 (cont.) (includes play-along section)

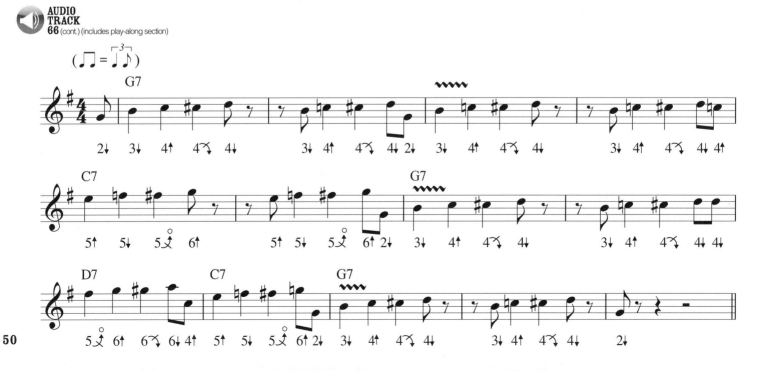

67 This is a nice lick with a little bounce back. Transposed, it works well over all three changes of the 12-bar. You will notice that it starts off with the basic ascending swing lick #1, before extending.

AUDIO
TRACK
67 (includes play-along section)

68 The next example fits nicely over a Latin beat. It transposes easily over the blues changes.

AUDIO
TRACK
68 (includes play-along section)

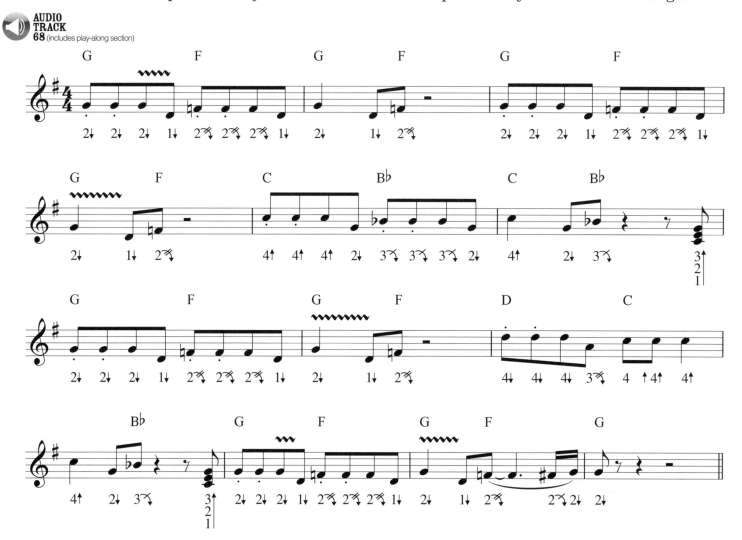

68A The previous lick is often played in 3rd position, or C harp in the key of D.
This lick is laid out pretty naturally for 3rd position.

AUDIO
TRACK
69 (includes play-along section)

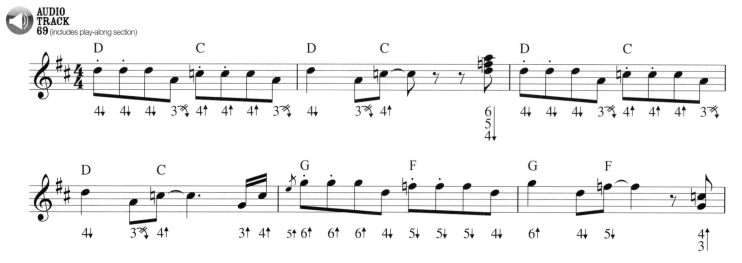

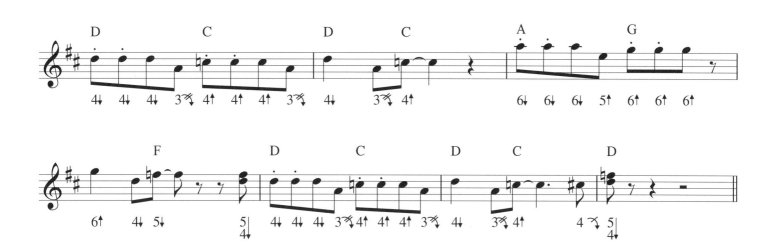

69 This is another great standard lick, and is usable as a full sounding background part, or as a stand-alone lick in many shuffle tunes. Slowed down, it works well on slow blues tunes.

AUDIO TRACK 70

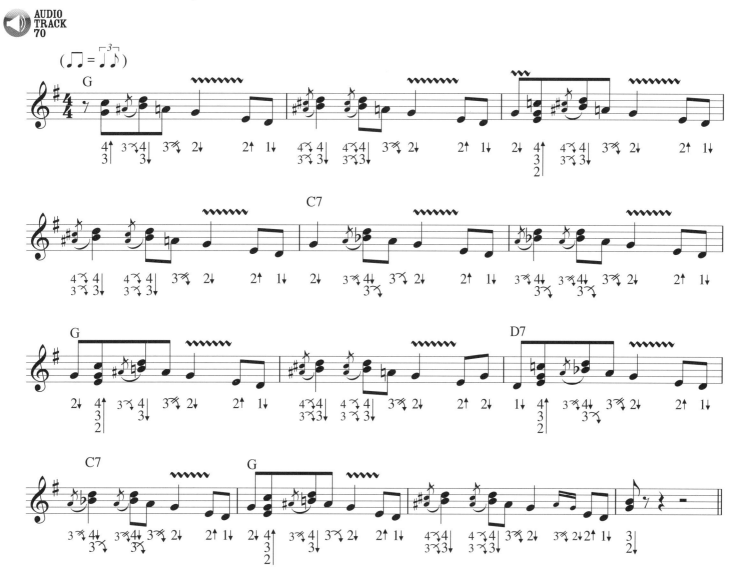

69A Melodically similar to the previous lick, the next example is a distinctive standard lick that gets used a lot. It could be used as a background motif in almost any shuffle or as a part of a solo, and works nicely over blues changes without alteration.

AUDIO TRACK
70 (cont.) (includes play-along section)

TURNAROUNDS AND ENDINGS

The turnaround section of a 12-bar blues progression encompasses all or part of the eleventh and twelfth bar. This is the part of the progression that forms either an ending to a verse, a bridge between verses, or an ending to the song. Here are some of the many licks that are used over this part of a blues progression. The background guitar parts on the demo tracks will start on what would be the ninth bar of a 12-bar progression. That spot in a 12-bar is sometimes called "coming down from the V chord." This same spot is sometimes used as an introduction at the beginning of a blues song.

70 This is an authentic and frequently used turnaround. It's actually two distinct turnaround licks that work well when played sequentially, but these could be separated and used independently.

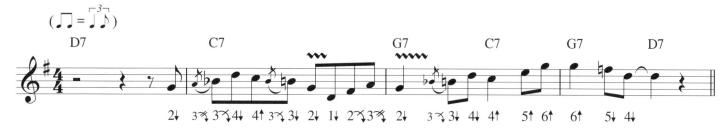

71 This standard turnaround can be used with almost any shuffle. It may have originated on guitar or bass, but plays nicely on harmonica.

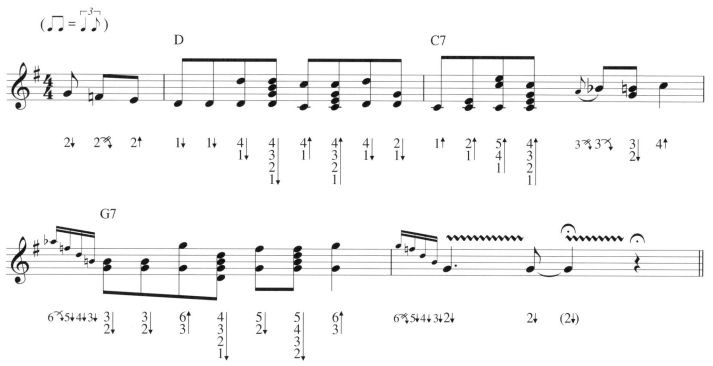

72 This is a classic turnaround lick that is usually played on the guitar, but works well on harmonica.

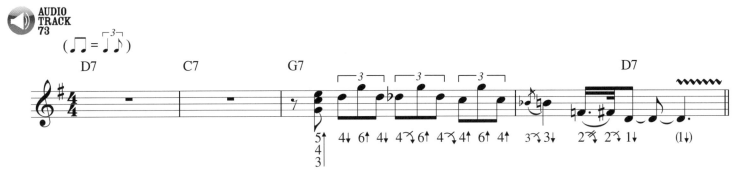

73 Little Walter used this distinctive ending often. It is very melodic and sounds different than many of the other blues turnarounds usually heard.

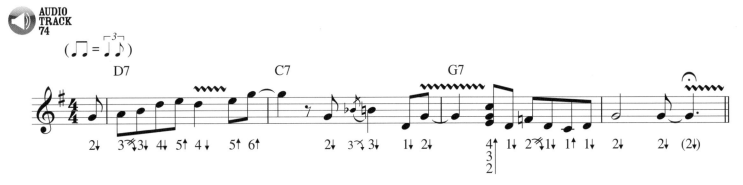

74 A favorite ending lick for Freddie King, this one-bar phrase translates well to the harp. It breaks time, which makes a nice contrast.

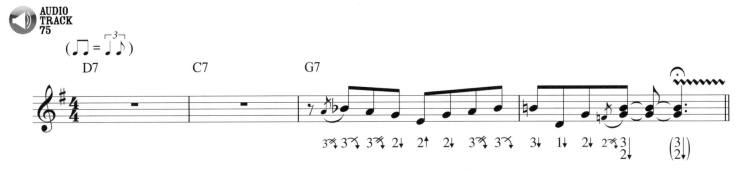

75 This one-bar ending lick works nicely over almost any blues shuffle tune. It was an ending lick that Sonny Boy Williamson used a lot.

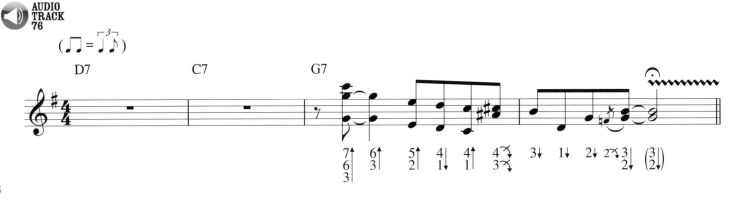

CHESS ERA LICKS

Many blues aficionados agree that the Chess record label recordings from the mid-1940s through the late 1950s helped frame one of the golden ages of post-war blues music. That time frame is frequently referred to as the Chess Era. Some of the following groups of licks originated or were popularized in that time period.

Most of the following licks are associated with songs that were frequently played by Chess era harmonica players like Sonny Boy Williamson, Little Walter, and Howlin' Wolf, even in cases where the licks were not actually played on the harmonica.

LICKS ASSOCIATED WITH SONNY BOY WILLIAMSON II SONGS

Sonny Boy recorded for numerous labels, but his most widely known songs were recorded for Chess. These are all-purpose licks that can be used in any number of blues songs. Some of them were used often by Sonny Boy Williamson II, but others are licks that Sonny Boy never played on the harmonica, and were used as background parts in some of his songs. They all fit nicely in many standard blues songs.

76 This lick and its variations are constructed of two triplets followed by two resolution notes. They can be dropped into a solo almost anywhere in a 12-bar. On the recorded example, the sequence is as follows: the basic lick is played, followed by a subtle variation, 76a, that has been adapted by bouncing down instead of up in the second triplet. The third variation, 76b, demonstrates how these two variations can be alternated and repeated for added interest.

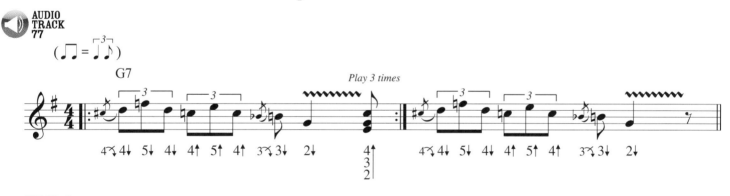

76A

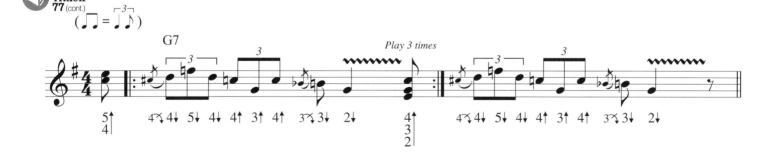

76B

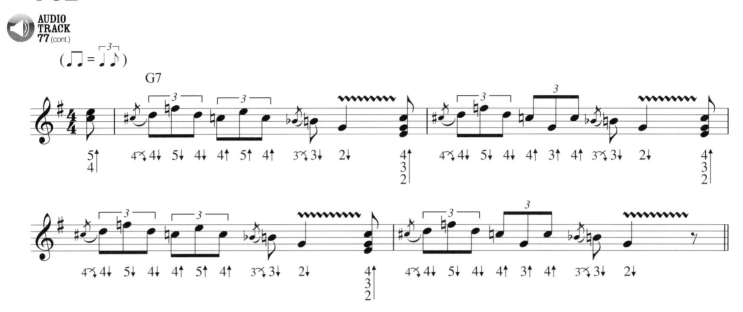

77 Here is another authentic, classic lick that was a part of Sonny Boy's bag of tricks. This lick is somewhat opposite the previous lick in that it begins with two pickup notes, followed by three triplets. The demonstration of it here is first played with the single-note pucker method and followed by the tongue-block version, which is how Sonny Boy would have played it.

78 Despite being the key lick in a Sonny Boy tune, Sonny Boy never actually played this on the harmonica; it was a background part. A staple lick that is often repeated, it works well in songs like "Green Onions," "Help Me," and "On the Road Again." It's one of the most widely quoted licks in all of blues. It is in a minor orientation.

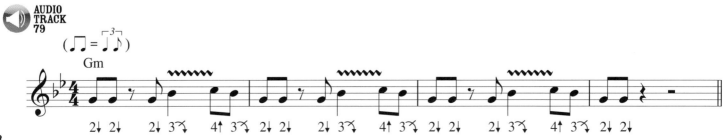

79 Here's a lick that works nicely with songs like "One Way Out," "Rockinitis," and "Who Do You Love." It is easily transposable, but sounds right and is often performed over all three changes of a 12-bar without modification.

AUDIO
TRACK
80

80 This is a lick that Sonny Boy used A LOT. It has been copied ad infinitum, and it is a must-know in the compendium of blues harmonica licks. At its most basic, this lick is a triplet with a little bend out of the second note. This is a great repeating lick that can be played over all the changes of a blues song without transposition, either as a stand-alone lick, or a repeating show stopper.

The example is first played as described above, then adapted by dropping the first unbent note of the triplet, and going straight to the bent note. Finally, the two versions are played alternately.

AUDIO
TRACK
81

LICKS ASSOCIATED WITH LITTLE WALTER SONGS

If it can be said that Chess records helped define one of the golden eras of blues music, it follows that Little Walter did more than his share to define blues harmonica playing in that era, and beyond. He made numerous recordings as a solo artist, but was also an in-demand accompanist. His style and licks are often copied, but have never been improved upon. While some of the following licks were played by Little Walter often, others just fit nicely with the songs that he played.

81 Here's a great lick that can be used as an intro lick, or anywhere in a solo, in part or in whole.

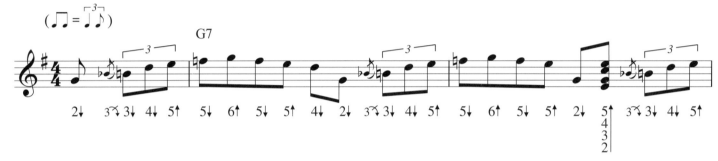

82 This is an all-purpose ascending lick that works well over the I chord.

83

This is a great slow blues lick. It can be used as an intro lick, or it stands alone as part of a solo. It provides a good example of how Little Walter would use syncopation and repeating notes to create his distinctive style.

AUDIO
TRACK
84

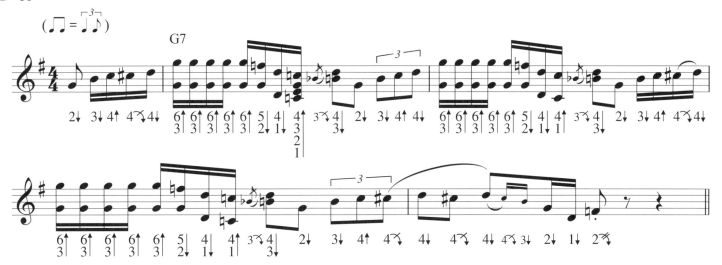

84

This classic lick contains a familiar descending phrase. It works nicely with songs like "I'm Goin' Down," "Everything's Going to Be All Right," and "Oh Baby."

It is appropriate to simulate mandolin style guitar picking in the beginning by continuously tonguing the first note. This technique is indicated by three diagonal lines on the note staff. This lick can be played over all the changes of a 12-bar without alteration.

AUDIO
TRACK
85 (includes play-along section)

85 This is a useful lick for descending from the top of the harp into a lower register. It works well as a bridge between licks when building a solo. This example is played in single notes.

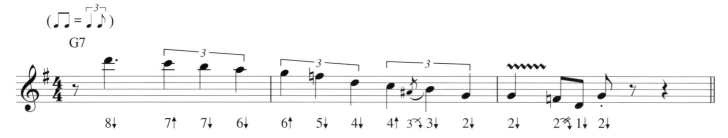

85A Lick 85 is played here using tongue-blocked chords in place of single notes.

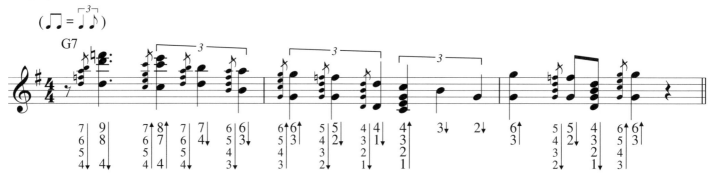

85B A different feel is created by employing a different rhythmic emphasis, even while playing the same notes. This example is played using tongue blocking.

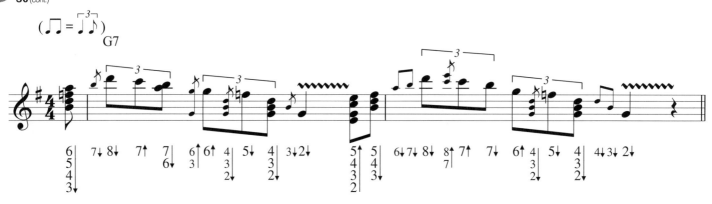

86 This lick works well over the I chord, but could be played over the other changes of a blues progression. It has the feel of a guitar or bass lick, but sounds great on harp.

87 This is a lick that works well with songs like "Sloppy Drunk," "Tell Me Mama," or "Crazy Mixed Up World." The example here is played with a combination of single-note puckers and tongue-block chords, with a little glissando at the end. There is some double-stop technique after the three introductory pickup notes.

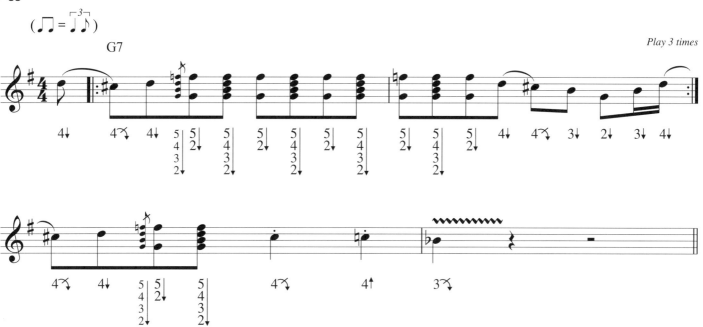

88

Here's a single-note lick that works well in a slow blues setting. This is another lick that demonstrates the unique kind of syncopation and trilling technique that Little Walter used, and is one reason his playing was so distinctive. In this example, the lick is first played with tongue blocking as Walter would have played it, then using the single-note pucker method.

89

Little Walter used this lick often. It's very similar to one that Sonny Boy Williamson I liked to use. This would also work well as a response lick to lick 94.

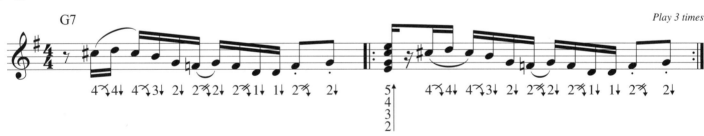

LICKS FROM SONGS ASSOCIATED WITH HOWLIN'WOLF

Most of the next group of licks were not played on the harmonica, but were used as background parts in Howlin' Wolf tunes. They are all authentic, stock licks that work well on the harmonica in a variety of shuffle tunes.

90 Although this is generally thought of as a standard bass or guitar part, it's a lick that makes a great backup part, or the basis for a solo on harmonica. It also transposes rather easily over the three chords of a 12-bar, and works well over songs like "Shake" and "Everybody's Got to Change Sometimes," among others.

AUDIO
TRACK
91 (includes play-along section)

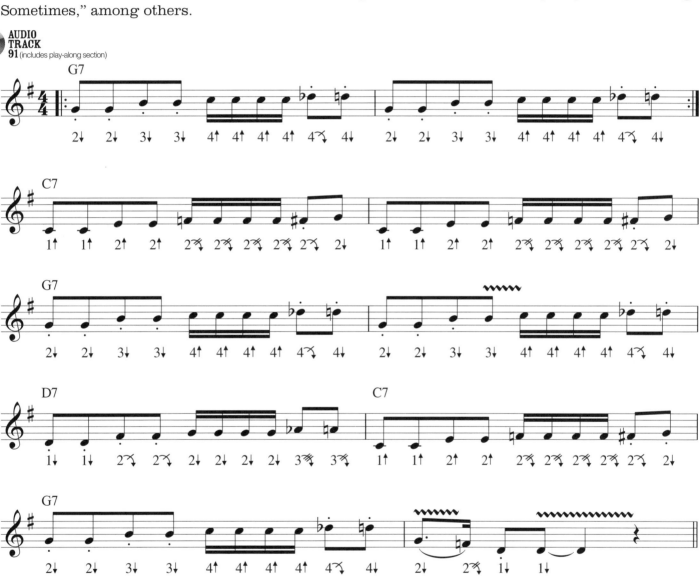

91 Here's another great lick that works well with the same group of songs as the previous lick. It's another universal lick that transposes easily over the chords of a blues progression. This example is played using mostly chords, but using single notes is an option.

AUDIO
TRACK
91 (cont.)

92 This classic lick works well on one-chord vamp tunes like "Smokestack Lightning" or "Moanin' at Midnight." It's another blues lick that probably originated on guitar, but translates well to the harmonica.

AUDIO
TRACK
92

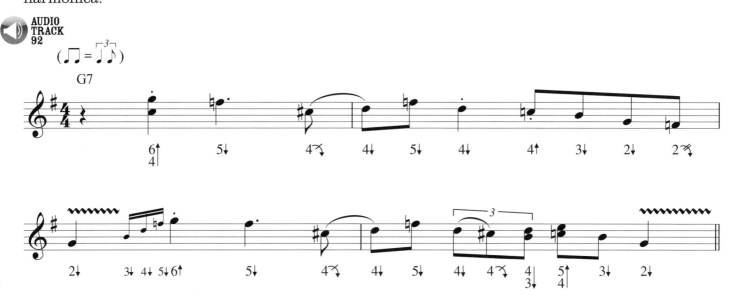

92A
You can shake up the previous lick a little bit by replacing the second note of the phrase with an over blow on the 6 hole.

93
This is a nice lick that works well over the I chord and also as a response lick in songs like "Forty-Four," "My Little Girl," or "One of These Mornings." Howlin' Wolf and Little Walter both used this lick.

93A Here is the previous lick in 3rd position, which is a great way to approach it, and a way that Little Walter often played it.

MISSISSIPPI DELTA GROOVE LICK

94 The sequence of phrases in this example works well with the family of songs that includes "Meet Me in the Bottom," "Rollin' and Tumblin'," "Diving Duck," "Traveling Riverside Blues," and "If I Had Possession over Judgment Day," among others. This is a call-and-response 12-bar form. The progression sometimes starts on the IV chord, as per this example. It can be played without adaptation over for the IV chord, but there is a slight alteration for playing over the V chord. It's one of the oldest blues patterns of all time.

LICKS FROM SONGS ASSOCIATED WITH JIMMY REED

Perhaps more than any other famous blues harp stylist, Jimmy Reed was known as a high note specialist. The simplicity of his playing was another hallmark that made his playing so well loved and often copied. Versions of the authentic licks that follow were frequently played by Jimmy Reed.

95
This lick works well with songs like "Big Boss Man;" "Memphis, Tennessee;" and many others. It makes a good introduction lick or launching point for a solo.

95A
Here's a 1st position version of the previous lick. Your C harmonica will now be played in the key of C. This works well as a turnaround, or over the I chord when playing in 1st position.

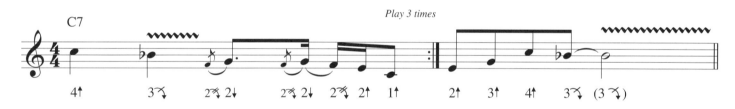

96
This next example works well with just about any mid-tempo shuffle, and works especially well over the I chord. It has a little trill in it.

HIGH NOTE 1ST POSITION LICKS

These licks are all played in 1st position, in the key of C on a C harp.

97 This triplet lick works best over the I chord. It works well in songs like "Honest I Do;" "Baby, What You Want Me to Do;" and "Bright Lights, Big City." Jimmy Reed used this lick and others like it.

97A The previous lick also works well when you move up one hole to play a harmony.

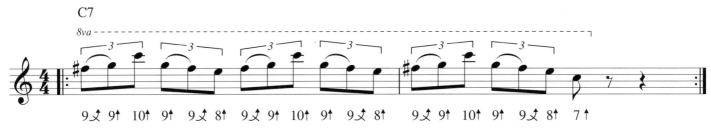

97B This triplet variation of the previous lick requires good control of the 10-hole second bend.

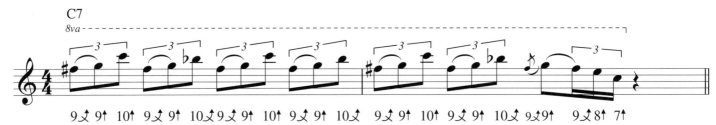

98

This short high-note lick gets played a lot. It makes a great accent lick. Adding a little vibrato to the end note helps bring it to life.

AUDIO
TRACK
97 (cont.)

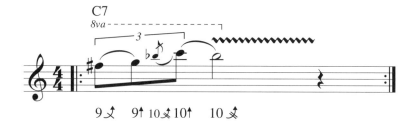

99

This lick can be used almost anywhere in a 12-bar, but works well as a turnaround lick.

AUDIO
TRACK
98

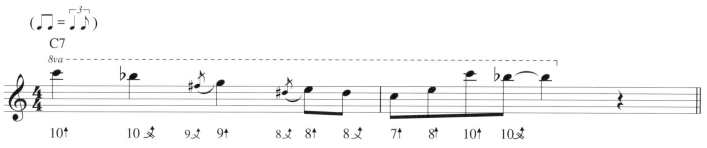

99A

The above lick also sounds good played on the low end in 1st position. It is a lick that James Cotton and Big Walter liked to play.

AUDIO
TRACK
98 (cont.)

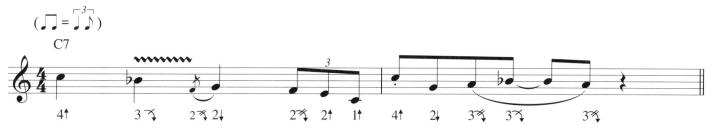

100 This is the classic guitar turnaround lick, similar to the 2nd position turnaround lick 72, but is played on the high notes in 1st position.

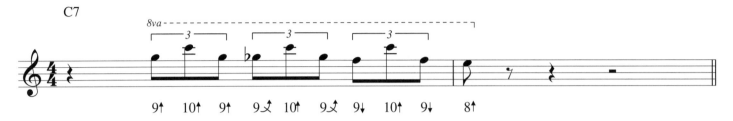

100A Here's the same lick played on the low notes in 1st position.

HARMONICA NOTATION LEGEND

Harmonica music can be notated two different ways: on a *musical staff*, and in *tablature*.

THE MUSICAL STAFF shows pitches and rhythms and is divided by bar lines into measures. Pitches are named after the first seven letters of the alphabet.

TABLATURE graphically represents the harmonica music. Each note will be accompanied by a number, 1 through 10, indicating what hole you are to play. The arrow that follows indicates whether to blow or draw. (All examples are shown using a C diatonic harmonica.)

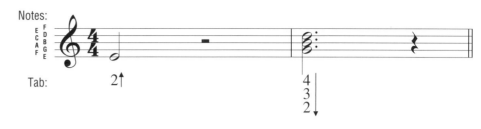

Blow (exhale) into 2nd hole.

Draw (inhale) 2nd, 3rd, & 4th holes together.

Notes on the C Harmonica

Exhaled (Blown) Notes

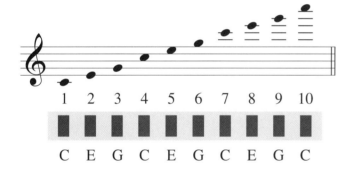

1	2	3	4	5	6	7	8	9	10
C	E	G	C	E	G	C	E	G	C

Inhaled (Drawn) Notes

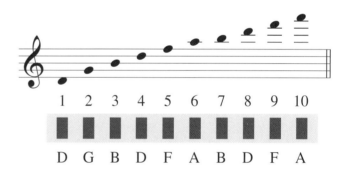

1	2	3	4	5	6	7	8	9	10
D	G	B	D	F	A	B	D	F	A

Bends

Blow Bends

- 1/4 step
- 1/2 step
- 1 step
- 1 1/2 steps

Draw Bends

- 1/4 step
- 1/2 step
- 1 step
- 1 1/2 steps

Definitions for Special Harmonica Notation

SLURRED BEND: Play (draw) 3rd hole, then bend the note down one whole step.

GRACE NOTE BEND: Starting with a pre-bent note, immediately release bend to the target note.

VIBRATO: Begin adding vibrato to the sustained note on beat 3.

TONGUE BLOCKING: Using your tongue to block holes 2 & 3, play octaves on holes 1 & 4.

TRILL: Shake the harmonica rapidly to alternate between notes.

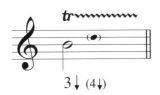

NOTE: Tablature numbers in parentheses are used when:

- The note is sustained, but a new articulation begins (such as vibrato), or
- The quantity of notes being sustained changes, or
- A change in dynamics (volume) occurs.
- It's the alternate note in a trill.

Additional Musical Definitions

D.S. al Coda

- Go back to the sign (%), then play until the measure marked "***To Coda,***" then skip to the section labelled "**Coda.**"

D.C. al Fine

- Go back to the beginning of the song and play until the measure marked "***Fine***" (end).

- Repeat measures between signs.

(accent)

- Accentuate the note (play initial attack louder).

(staccato)

- Play the note short.

- When a repeated section has different endings, play the first ending only the first time and the second ending only the second time.

Dynamics

p
- Piano (soft)

mp
- Mezzo Piano (medium soft)

mf
- Mezzo Forte (medium loud)

f
- Forte (loud)

(crescendo)
- Gradually louder

(decrescendo)
- Gradually softer

THE HAL LEONARD HARMONICA METHOD AND SONGBOOKS

THE METHOD

THE HAL LEONARD COMPLETE HARMONICA METHOD — CHROMATIC HARMONICA
by Bobby Joe Holman

The only harmonica method to present the chromatic harmonica in 14 scales and modes in all 12 keys! This book/CD pack will take beginners from the basics on through to the most advanced techniques available for the contemporary harmonica player. Each section contains appropriate songs and exercises (which are demonstrated on the CD) that enable the player to quickly learn the various concepts presented. Every aspect of this versatile musical instrument is explored and explained in easy-to-understand detail with illustrations. The musical styles covered include traditional, blues, pop and rock.

00841286 Book/CD Pack $12.95

THE HAL LEONARD COMPLETE HARMONICA METHOD — DIATONIC HARMONICA
by Bobby Joe Holman

The only harmonica method specific to the diatonic harmonica, covering all six positions. This book/CD pack contains over 20 songs and musical examples that take beginners from the basics on through to the most advanced techniques available for the contemporary harmonica player. Each section contains appropriate songs and exercises (which are demonstrated on the CD) that enable the player to quickly learn the various concepts presented. Every aspect of this versatile musical instrument is explored and explained in easy-to-understand detail with illustrations. The musical styles covered include traditional, blues, pop and rock.

00841285 Book/CD Pack $12.95

THE SONGBOOKS

The Hal Leonard Harmonica Songbook series offers a wide variety of music especially tailored to the two-volume Hal Leonard Harmonica Method, but can be played by all harmonica players, diatonic and chromatic alike. All books include study and performance notes, and a guide to harmonica tablature. From classical themes to Christmas music, rock and roll to Broadway, there's something for everyone!

BROADWAY SONGS FOR HARMONICA
INCLUDES TAB
arranged by Bobby Joe Holman

19 show-stopping Broadway tunes for the harmonica. Songs include: Ain't Misbehavin' • Bali Ha'i • Camelot • Climb Ev'ry Mountain • Do-Re-Mi • Edelweiss • Give My Regards to Broadway • Hello, Dolly! • I've Grown Accustomed to Her Face • The Impossible Dream (The Quest) • Memory • Oklahoma • People • and more.

00820009 .... $9.95

CLASSICAL FAVORITES FOR HARMONICA
INCLUDES TAB
arranged by Bobby Joe Holman

18 famous classical melodies and themes, arranged for diatonic and chromatic players. Includes: By the Beautiful Blue Danube • Clair De Lune • The Flight of the Bumble Bee • Gypsy Rondo • Moonlight Sonata • Surprise Symphony • The Swan (Le Cygne) • Waltz of the Flowers • and more, plus a guide to harmonica tablature.

00820006 .... $9.95

MOVIE FAVORITES FOR HARMONICA
INCLUDES TAB
arranged by Bobby Joe Holman

19 songs from the silver screen, arranged for diatonic and chromatic harmonica. Includes: Alfie • Bless the Beasts and Children • Chim Chim Cher-ee • The Entertainer • Georgy Girl • Midnight Cowboy • Moon River • Picnic • Speak Softly, Love • Stormy Weather • Tenderly • Unchained Melody • What a Wonderful World • and more, plus a guide to harmonica tablature.

00820014 .... $9.95

POP ROCK FAVORITES FOR HARMONICA
INCLUDES TAB
arranged by Bobby Joe Holman

17 classic hits especially arranged for harmonica (either diatonic or chromatic), including: Abraham, Martin and John • All I Have to Do Is Dream • Blueberry Hill • Daydream • Runaway • Sixteen Candles • Sleepwalk • Something • Stand by Me • Tears on My Pillow • Tell It like It Is • Yakety Yak • and more.

00820013 .... $9.95

Prices, contents and availability subject to change without notice.

FOR MORE INFORMATION, SEE YOUR LOCAL MUSIC DEALER, OR WRITE TO:

HAL•LEONARD® CORPORATION
7777 W. BLUEMOUND RD. P.O. BOX 13819 MILWAUKEE, WI 53213

Visit Hal Leonard Online at
www.halleonard.com

HAL·LEONARD BLUES PLAY-ALONG

For use with all the C, B♭, Bass Clef and E♭ Instruments, the Hal Leonard Blues Play-Along Series is the ultimate jamming tool for all blues musicians.

With easy-to-read lead sheets, and other split-track choices on the included CD, these first-of-a-kind packages will bring your local blues jam right into your house! Each song on the CD includes two tracks: a full stereo mix, and a split track mix with removable guitar, bass, piano, and harp parts. The CD is playable on any CD player, and is also enhanced so Mac and PC users can adjust the recording to any tempo without changing the pitch!

1. Chicago Blues
All Your Love (I Miss Loving) • Easy Baby • I Ain't Got You • I'm Your Hoochie Coochie Man • Killing Floor • Mary Had a Little Lamb • Messin' with the Kid • Sweet Home Chicago.
00843106 Book/CD Pack $12.99

2. Texas Blues
Hide Away • If You Love Me Like You Say • Mojo Hand • Okie Dokie Stomp • Pride and Joy • Reconsider Baby • T-Bone Shuffle • The Things That I Used to Do.
00843107 Book/CD Pack $12.99

3. Slow Blues
Don't Throw Your Love on Me So Strong • Five Long Years • I Can't Quit You Baby • I Just Want to Make Love to You • The Sky Is Crying • (They Call It) Stormy Monday (Stormy Monday Blues) • Sweet Little Angel • Texas Flood.
00843108 Book/CD Pack $12.99

4. Shuffle Blues
Beautician Blues • Bright Lights, Big City • Further on up the Road • I'm Tore Down • Juke • Let Me Love You Baby • Look at Little Sister • Rock Me Baby.
00843171 Book/CD Pack $12.99

5. B.B. King
Everyday I Have the Blues • It's My Own Fault Darlin' • Just Like a Woman • Please Accept My Love • Sweet Sixteen • The Thrill Is Gone • Why I Sing the Blues • You Upset Me Baby.
00843172 Book/CD Pack $14.99

6. Jazz Blues
Birk's Works • Blues in the Closet • Cousin Mary • Freddie Freeloader • Now's the Time • Tenor Madness • Things Ain't What They Used to Be • Turnaround.
00843175 Book/CD Pack $12.99

7. Howlin' Wolf
Built for Comfort • Forty-Four • How Many More Years • Killing Floor • Moanin' at Midnight • Shake for Me • Sitting on Top of the World • Smokestack Lightning.
00843176 Book/CD Pack $12.99

8. Blues Classics
Baby, Please Don't Go • Boom Boom • Born Under a Bad Sign • Dust My Broom • How Long, How Long Blues • I Ain't Superstitious • It Hurts Me Too • My Babe.
00843177 Book/CD Pack $12.99

9. Albert Collins
Brick • Collins' Mix • Don't Lose Your Cool • Frost Bite • Frosty • I Ain't Drunk • Master Charge • Trash Talkin'.
00843178 Book/CD Pack $12.99

10. Uptempo Blues
Cross Road Blues (Crossroads) • Give Me Back My Wig • Got My Mo Jo Working • The House Is Rockin' • Paying the Cost to Be the Boss • Rollin' and Tumblin' • Turn on Your Love Light • You Can't Judge a Book by the Cover.
00843179 Book/CD Pack $12.99

11. Christmas Blues
Back Door Santa • Blue Christmas • Dig That Crazy Santa Claus • Merry Christmas, Baby • Please Come Home for Christmas • Santa Baby • Soulful Christmas.
00843203 Book/CD Pack $12.99

12. Jimmy Reed
Ain't That Lovin' You Baby • Baby, What You Want Me to Do • Big Boss Man • Bright Lights, Big City • Going to New York • Honest I Do • You Don't Have to Go • You Got Me Dizzy.
00843204 Book/CD Pack $12.99

1111

Presenting the Hal Leonard JAZZ PLAY-ALONG® SERIES

For use with all B-flat, E-flat, Bass Clef and C instruments, the Jazz Play-Along® Series is the ultimate learning tool for all jazz musicians. With musician-friendly lead sheets, melody cues, and other split-track choices on the included CD, these first-of-a-kind packages help you master improvisation while playing some of the greatest tunes of all time. FOR STUDY, each tune includes a split track with: melody cue with proper style and inflection • professional rhythm tracks • choruses for soloing • removable bass part • removable piano part. FOR PERFORMANCE, each tune also has: an additional full stereo accompaniment track (no melody) • additional choruses for soloing.

73. JAZZ/BLUES
   00843075.....................$14.95

74. BEST JAZZ CLASSICS
   00843076.....................$15.99

75. PAUL DESMOND
   00843077.....................$16.99

76. BROADWAY JAZZ BALLADS
   00843078.....................$15.99

77. JAZZ ON BROADWAY
   00843079.....................$15.99

78. STEELY DAN
   00843070.....................$15.99

79. MILES DAVIS CLASSICS
   00843081.....................$15.99

80. JIMI HENDRIX
   00843083.....................$16.99

81. FRANK SINATRA – CLASSICS
   00843084.....................$15.99

82. FRANK SINATRA – STANDARDS
   00843085.....................$16.99

83. ANDREW LLOYD WEBBER
   00843104.....................$14.95

84. BOSSA NOVA CLASSICS
   00843105.....................$14.95

85. MOTOWN HITS
   00843109.....................$14.95

86. BENNY GOODMAN
   00843110.....................$15.99

87. DIXIELAND
   00843111.....................$16.99

88. DUKE ELLINGTON FAVORITES
   00843112.....................$14.95

89. IRVING BERLIN FAVORITES
   00843113.....................$14.95

90. THELONIOUS MONK CLASSICS
   00841262.....................$16.99

91. THELONIOUS MONK FAVORITES
   00841263.....................$16.99

92. LEONARD BERNSTEIN
   00450134.....................$15.99

93. DISNEY FAVORITES
   00843142.....................$14.99

94. RAY
   00843143.....................$14.99

95. JAZZ AT THE LOUNGE
   00843144.....................$14.99

96. LATIN JAZZ STANDARDS
   00843145.....................$15.99

97. MAYBE I'M AMAZED*
   00843148.....................$15.99

98. DAVE FRISHBERG
   00843149.....................$15.99

99. SWINGING STANDARDS
   00843150.....................$14.99

100. LOUIS ARMSTRONG
   00740423.....................$16.99

101. BUD POWELL
   00843152.....................$14.99

102. JAZZ POP
   00843153.....................$15.99

103. ON GREEN DOLPHIN STREET
    & OTHER JAZZ CLASSICS
   00843154.....................$14.99

104. ELTON JOHN
   00843155.....................$14.99

105. SOULFUL JAZZ
   00843151.....................$15.99

106. SLO' JAZZ
   00843117.....................$14.99

107. MOTOWN CLASSICS
   00843116.....................$14.99

108. JAZZ WALTZ
   00843159.....................$15.99

109. OSCAR PETERSON
   00843160.....................$16.99

110. JUST STANDARDS
   00843161.....................$15.99

111. COOL CHRISTMAS
   00843162.....................$15.99

112. PAQUITO D'RIVERA – LATIN JAZZ*
   48020662.....................$16.99

113. PAQUITO D'RIVERA – BRAZILIAN JAZZ*
   48020663.....................$19.99

114. MODERN JAZZ QUARTET FAVORITES
   00843163.....................$15.99

115. THE SOUND OF MUSIC
   00843164.....................$15.99

116. JACO PASTORIUS
   00843165.....................$15.99

117. ANTONIO CARLOS JOBIM – MORE HITS
   00843166.....................$15.99

118. BIG JAZZ STANDARDS COLLECTION
   00843167.....................$27.50

119. JELLY ROLL MORTON
   00843168.....................$15.99

120. J.S. BACH
   00843169.....................$15.99

121. DJANGO REINHARDT
   00843170.....................$15.99

122. PAUL SIMON
   00843182.....................$16.99

123. BACHARACH & DAVID
   00843185.....................$15.99

124. JAZZ-ROCK HORN HITS
   00843186.....................$15.99

126. COUNT BASIE CLASSICS
   00843157.....................$15.99

127. CHUCK MANGIONE
   00843188.....................$15.99

128. VOCAL STANDARDS (LOW VOICE)
   00843189.....................$15.99

129. VOCAL STANDARDS (HIGH VOICE)
   00843190.....................$15.99

130. VOCAL JAZZ (LOW VOICE)
   00843191.....................$15.99

131. VOCAL JAZZ (HIGH VOICE)
   00843192.....................$15.99

132. STAN GETZ ESSENTIALS
   00843193.....................$15.99

133. STAN GETZ FAVORITES
   00843194.....................$15.99

134. NURSERY RHYMES*
   00843196.....................$17.99

135. JEFF BECK
   00843197.....................$15.99

136. NAT ADDERLEY
   00843198.....................$15.99

137. WES MONTGOMERY
   00843199.....................$15.99

138. FREDDIE HUBBARD
   00843200.....................$15.99

139. JULIAN "CANNONBALL" ADDERLEY
   00843201.....................$15.99

140. JOE ZAWINUL
   00843202.....................$15.99

141. BILL EVANS STANDARDS
   00843156.....................$15.99

142. CHARLIE PARKER GEMS
   00843222.....................$15.99

143. JUST THE BLUES
   00843223.....................$15.99

144. LEE MORGAN
   00843229.....................$15.99

145. COUNTRY STANDARDS
   00843230.....................$15.99

146. RAMSEY LEWIS
   00843231.....................$15.99

147. SAMBA
   00843232.....................$15.99

150. JAZZ IMPROV BASICS
   00843195.....................$19.99

151. MODERN JAZZ QUARTET CLASSICS
   00843209.....................$15.99

152. J.J. JOHNSON
   00843210.....................$15.99

154. HENRY MANCINI
   00843213.....................$14.99

155. SMOOTH JAZZ CLASSICS
   00843215.....................$15.99

156. THELONIOUS MONK – EARLY GEMS
   00843216.....................$15.99

157. HYMNS
   00843217.....................$15.99

158. JAZZ COVERS ROCK
   00843219.....................$15.99

159. MOZART
   00843220.....................$15.99

160. GEORGE SHEARING
   14041531.....................$16.99

161. DAVE BRUBECK
   14041556 ....$16.99

162. BIG CHRISTMAS COLLECTION
   00843221.....................$24.99

164. HERB ALPERT
   14041775 ....$16.99

165. GEORGE BENSON
   00843240.....................$16.99

167. JOHNNY MANDEL
   00103642.....................$16.99

168. TADD DAMERON
   00103663.....................$15.99

169. BEST JAZZ STANDARDS
   00109249.....................$19.99

170. ULTIMATE JAZZ STANDARDS
   00109250.....................$19.99

172. POP STANDARDS
   00111669.....................$15.99

174. TIN PAN ALLEY
   00119125.....................$15.99

175. TANGO
   00119836.....................$15.99

176. JOHNNY MERCER
   00119838.....................$15.99

HAL•LEONARD®
CORPORATION
7777 W. BLUEMOUND RD. P.O. BOX 13819
MILWAUKEE, WISCONSIN 53213

For complete songlists and more,
visit Hal Leonard online at
www.halleonard.com

1013

*These CDs do not include split tracks.

THE ULTIMATE COLLECTION OF
FAKE BOOKS

The Real Book – Sixth Edition

Hal Leonard proudly presents the first legitimate and legal editions of these books ever produced. These bestselling titles are mandatory for anyone who plays jazz! Over 400 songs, including: All By Myself • Dream a Little Dream of Me • God Bless the Child • Like Someone in Love • When I Fall in Love • and more.

00240221	Volume 1, C Edition	$35.00
00240224	Volume 1, B♭ Edition	$35.00
00240225	Volume 1, E♭ Edition	$35.00
00240226	Volume 1, BC Edition	$35.00
00240222	Volume 2, C Edition	$35.00
00240227	Volume 2, B♭ Edition	$35.00
00240228	Volume 2, E♭ Edition	$35.00

Best Fake Book Ever – 4th Edition

More than 1,000 songs from all styles of music, including: All My Loving • At the Hop • Cabaret • Dust in the Wind • Fever • From a Distance • Hello, Dolly! • Hey Jude • King of the Road • Longer • Misty • Route 66 • Sentimental Journey • Somebody • Song Sung Blue • Spinning Wheel • Unchained Melody • We Will Rock You • What a Wonderful World • Wooly Bully • Y.M.C.A. • and more.

00290239	C Edition	$49.99
00240083	B♭ Edition	$49.95
00240084	E♭ Edition	$49.95

Classic Rock Fake Book – 2nd Edition

This fake book is a great compilation of more than 250 terrific songs of the rock era, arranged for piano, voice, guitar and all C instruments. Includes: All Right Now • American Woman • Birthday • Honesty • I Shot the Sheriff • I Want You to Want Me • Imagine • It's Still Rock and Roll to Me • Lay Down Sally • Layla • My Generation • Rock and Roll All Nite • Spinning Wheel • White Room • We Will Rock You • lots more!

00240108 ....$32.50

Classical Fake Book – 2nd Edition

This unprecedented, amazingly comprehensive reference includes over 850 classical themes and melodies for all classical music lovers. Includes everything from Renaissance music to Vivaldi and Mozart to Mendelssohn. Lyrics in the original language are included when appropriate.

00240044 ....$37.50

The Disney Fake Book – 3rd Edition

Over 200 of the most beloved songs of all time, including: Be Our Guest • Can You Feel the Love Tonight • Colors of the Wind • Cruella De Vil • Friend Like Me • Heigh-Ho • It's a Small World • Mickey Mouse March • Supercalifragilisticexpialidocious • Under the Sea • When You Wish upon a Star • A Whole New World • Zip-A-Dee-Doo-Dah • and more!

00240039 ....$30.00

The Folksong Fake Book

Over 1,000 folksongs perfect for performers, school teachers, and hobbyists. Includes: Bury Me Not on the Lone Prairie • Clementine • Danny Boy • The Erie Canal • Go, Tell It on the Mountain • Home on the Range • Kumbaya • Michael Row the Boat Ashore • Shenandoah • Simple Gifts • Swing Low, Sweet Chariot • When Johnny Comes Marching Home • Yankee Doodle • and many more.

00240151 ....$24.95

The Hymn Fake Book

Nearly 1,000 multi-denominational hymns perfect for church musicians or hobbyists: Amazing Grace • Christ the Lord Is Risen Today • For the Beauty of the Earth • It Is Well with My Soul • A Mighty Fortress Is Our God • O for a Thousand Tongues to Sing • Praise to the Lord, the Almighty • Take My Life and Let It Be • What a Friend We Have in Jesus • and hundreds more!

00240145 ....$24.95

The Praise & Worship Fake Book

400 songs: As the Deer • Better Is One Day • Come, Now Is the Time to Worship • Firm Foundation • Glorify Thy Name • Here I Am to Worship • I Could Sing of Your Love Forever • Lord, I Lift Your Name on High • More Precious Than Silver • Open the Eyes of My Heart • The Power of Your Love • Shine, Jesus, Shine • Trading My Sorrows • We Fall Down • You Are My All in All • and more.

00240234 ....$34.95

The R&B Fake Book – 2nd Edition

This terrific fake book features 375 classic R&B hits: Baby Love • Best of My Love • Dancing in the Street • Easy • Get Ready • Heatwave • Here and Now • Just Once • Let's Get It On • The Loco-Motion • (You Make Me Feel Like) A Natural Woman • One Sweet Day • Papa Was a Rollin' Stone • Save the Best for Last • September • Sexual Healing • Shop Around • Still • Tell It Like It Is • Up on the Roof • Walk on By • What's Going On • more!

00240107 C Edition $29.95

Ultimate Broadway Fake Book – 5th Edition

More than 700 show-stoppers from over 200 shows! Includes: Ain't Misbehavin' • All I Ask of You • Bewitched • Camelot • Don't Cry for Me Argentina • Edelweiss • I Dreamed a Dream • If I Were a Rich Man • Memory • Oklahoma • Send in the Clowns • What I Did for Love • more.

00240046 ....$49.99

FOR MORE INFORMATION, SEE YOUR LOCAL MUSIC DEALER, OR WRITE TO:

HAL•LEONARD® CORPORATION

7777 W. BLUEMOUND RD. P.O. BOX 13819 MILWAUKEE, WI 53213

Complete songlists available online at
www.halleonard.com

The Ultimate Christmas Fake Book – 5th Edition

This updated edition includes 275 traditional and contemporary Christmas songs: Away in a Manger • The Christmas Song • Deck the Hall • Frosty the Snow Man • A Holly Jolly Christmas • I Heard the Bells on Christmas Day • Jingle Bells • Little Saint Nick • Merry Christmas, Darling • Nuttin' for Christmas • Rudolph the Red-Nosed Reindeer • Silent Night • What Child Is This? • more.

00240045 ....$24.95

The Ultimate Country Fake Book – 5th Edition

This book includes over 700 of your favorite country hits: Always on My Mind • Boot Scootin' Boogie • Crazy • Down at the Twist and Shout • Forever and Ever, Amen • Friends in Low Places • The Gambler • Jambalaya • King of the Road • Sixteen Tons • There's a Tear in My Beer • Your Cheatin' Heart • and hundreds more.

00240049 ....$49.99

The Ultimate Fake Book – 5th Edition

Includes over 1,200 hits: Blue Skies • Body and Soul • Endless Love • Isn't It Romantic? • Memory • Mona Lisa • Moon River • Operator • Piano Man • Roxanne • Satin Doll • Shout • Small World • Smile • Speak Softly, Love • Strawberry Fields Forever • Tears in Heaven • Unforgettable • hundreds more!

00240024	C Edition	$49.95
00240026	B♭ Edition	$49.95
00240025	E♭ Edition	$49.95

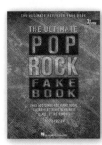

The Ultimate Pop/Rock Fake Book – 4th Edition

Over 600 pop standards and contemporary hits, including: All Shook Up • Another One Bites the Dust • Crying • Don't Know Much • Dust in the Wind • Earth Angel • Every Breath You Take • Hero • Hey Jude • Hold My Hand • Imagine • Layla • The Loco-Motion • Oh, Pretty Woman • On Broadway • Spinning Wheel • Stand by Me • Stayin' Alive • Tears in Heaven • True Colors • The Twist • Vision of Love • A Whole New World • Wild Thing • Wooly Bully • Yesterday • more!

00240099 ....$39.99

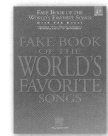

Fake Book of the World's Favorite Songs – 4th Edition

Over 700 favorites, including: America the Beautiful • Anchors Aweigh • Battle Hymn of the Republic • Bill Bailey, Won't You Please Come Home • Chopsticks • Für Elise • His Eye Is on the Sparrow • I Wonder Who's Kissing Her Now • Jesu, Joy of Man's Desiring • My Old Kentucky Home • Sidewalks of New York • Take Me Out to the Ball Game • When the Saints Go Marching In • and hundreds more!

00240072 ....$22.95